CW00428222

God's Great Plan

Published by
RICKFORDS HILL PUBLISHING LTD.
P.O. Box 576, Aylesbury, Buckinghamshire. HP22 6XX

First Published 2004

ISBN 1–905044–00–3

Typeset by Avocet Typeset, Chilton, Aylesbury,
Buckinghamshire.

Cover Design by Artset Graphics Ltd., Chesham,
Buckinghamshire.

Printed and bound in England by William Clowes,
Beccles, Suffolk.

God's Great Plan

By Damaris Harrison

Illustrations by Christine Fuller

Rickfords Hill Publishing

Note to parents

The message of God's good news can be
grasped by any child capable of following a
simple story. Indeed, many adults can testify
to having come to know Jesus Christ at a very
young age. For this reason, it is important to
teach children not only stories from the Bible,
but the great message of the Bible: God's
Great Plan of salvation. This book aims to
pass on that message in a way that is clear and
understandable to even the youngest child.
Bible references can be found at the back
of the book.

In the beginning
GOD

In the beginning God created the world.

He created the heavens and the earth and the sea,

the trees and the flowers,

the sun, the moon
and the stars,

the animals and
the birds,

and a daddy and a
mummy called Adam
and Eve.

Adam and Eve lived in the wonderful garden that God had made. There were beautiful flowers to smell and delicious fruit to eat.

Adam and Eve played with the animals. They could stroke the lion's velvet nose. They could pat the tiger's stripy head.

The birds and the butterflies flew and fluttered.

They were all very happy.

Every day God came and talked to Adam and Eve in the garden. He was their Friend.

God said,
'I want you to look after
the garden. I want you to
enjoy the delicious fruit of
all the trees in the garden,

except one.

You must not eat the fruit of this tree or you will die'.

Adam and Eve had a lovely time in the garden and God was their Friend.

But one day Adam and Eve disobeyed God. They ate some fruit from the special tree.

Oh dear!

God had to punish Adam and Eve. God said, 'You cannot stay in the garden any more because you did not obey Me. You must go out into the wide world'.

God was very sad that He had to punish Adam and Eve. He still loved them very much. God made them some special clothes to wear in the wide world.

God said, 'I have a plan to make Adam and Eve My friends again'.

Hooray!

Adam and Eve had some children and some grandchildren and some great grandchildren.
We all belong to Adam's Family, you and I.

Adam's family tried to obey God and be friends with Him again.

God made some rules for all His people. He said, 'You must love Me more than anyone else. You must be kind to all the people. Children, you must do as your mummy and daddy tell you. You must not take things that belong to other people.'

The people could not keep the rules. They had forgotten how to be friends with God.

Oh dear!

But God still had a plan to make the people His friends again.

God said,
'I will send My Son Jesus
down from heaven to the
people. He will live like them
in the wide world'.

Hooray!
Hooray!

So Jesus came to live
in the wide world.
He kept all the rules.
He never disobeyed God.
Because God was His Father,
Jesus was good, loving and
kind.

When the people said, 'We are sorry we cannot keep Your rules', Jesus said, 'I forgive you'.

Jesus made the poorly people better. He made the blind people see again. He made the deaf people hear again. Anyone who was poorly could ask Jesus to make him better.

But God said,
'I still have to punish the people because they disobeyed Me and broke My rules'.

Oh dear!

But God loved the people
very much. He said,
'Jesus hasn't broken any of
the rules. I will punish Jesus
and let the people go free'.

Jesus said,
'Yes, You can punish Me
instead of the people'.

So Jesus was punished instead of the people. They nailed Him to a wooden cross.
He died.
They put Him in a grave.

Oh dear!

The people that loved
Jesus were very sad.

But Jesus didn't stay dead.

He came alive again.

Hooray!

Hooray!

The people that loved
Jesus were very glad.

God said,
'Everyone that says "I'm sorry I broke Your rules", and everyone that says "Thank You God for punishing Jesus instead of me" can be friends with Me again.

'They will live with Me for ever and ever. I will forget that they ever disobeyed Me'.

Thank You Lord Jesus for being punished instead of me. I want to live with You for ever and ever.

All the truths taught in this book come from the Bible and can be found in the following places:

Creation and the garden: Genesis ch.1 & 2, particularly ch. 1:1, 11, 20–28; ch. 2:16–20

Adam and Eve disobey God: Genesis ch. 3, particularly verses 6, 21, 24

Adam and Eve's family: Genesis ch. 5; ch. 3:20

Adam's family unable to obey God: Genesis ch. 4:1–15, ch. 6:5, 6

God gives some rules: Exodus 20:1–17

People couldn't keep the rules: Psalm 14; Isaiah 64:6–7; Romans 7:14–23

God promises and sends His Son: Isaiah 7:14; Luke 2:11, 12

Jesus lives on earth: Luke 2:40; 1 Peter 2:21–23; Mark 2:5; Matthew 4:24

Jesus dies for the people: Isaiah 53:5, 6; John 10:17, 18; 19:16–19, 30; 20:11

Jesus comes alive again. John 20:12–20 Matthew 28:5–8

How we can be forgiven: Psalm 103:8–17; John 3:16; 5:24; Acts 2:21, 37–39; John 20:31

To purchase further copies of this book or to find out about other titles available, please visit our web-site at www.rhpbooks.co.uk or write to us for a leaflet enclosing a stamped self-addressed envelope:

Rickfords Hill Publishing Ltd., P.O. Box 576, Aylesbury. HP22 6XX